G A Z A – Graves, Ashes, Zeal, Ascension

Poems of Occupation, Resistance, and Return

Hashim K T

BookLeaf Publishing
India | USA | UK

Made with ❤ on the BookLeaf Publishing Platform
www.bookleafpub.in
www.bookleafpub.com

Dedication

To the pure souls of Gaza —

the women and children who met their Lord with hearts unbroken.

"Do not think of those who are slain in the way of God as dead.
They are alive, sustained by their Lord."
— Qur'an 3:169

Preface

G A Z A — Graves, Ashes, Zeal, Ascension

There are lands that tell their stories through monuments and museums.
And there are lands — like Gaza — that tell their stories through **graves and dust**, through the breath of widows and the silence of children.
Gaza is not a name written in geography.
It is a cry etched in eternity —
a city where the sea listens,
where every wave returns with a name that once laughed, once dreamed, once lived.
In Gaza, **the past** never sleeps; it stands beside the living.
The **Nakba** was not a single night of exile —
it became a lifetime of waiting, a history written in the language of loss.
The **present** burns, yet breathes —
a rhythm of sirens, prayers, and steadfast hearts that refuse surrender.
And the **future** — though wrapped in smoke — still glows
in the eyes of a child who draws the word *home* on the wall of a ruin.
This book is born from that dust.
Each poem is a witness —

to grief that has outlived generations,
to mothers who plant hope in the ashes,
to faith that rises each dawn despite the siege.
The letters of **G A Z A** hold the journey of a nation:
Graves, where memory sleeps;
Ashes, where homes once stood;
Zeal, that unbroken flame of the heart;
and **Ascension**, the promise that beyond every night lies
the call of God —
that no sacrifice is unseen,
and no martyr forgotten.
Let these poems speak where the world fell silent.
Let them carry the whispers of children,
the prayers of mothers,
and the steadfast echo of a people who still believe that
light belongs to those who refuse darkness.
For Gaza lives —
in the dust, in the dawn,
in every soul that still dares to say:
We are here.

Acknowledgements

The poems in *Gaza: The Stones Remember and Other Poems* draw their soul from the lived history and enduring faith of the Palestinian people. Though poetic in form, they echo real events, struggles, and voices of truth.

Sources of Inspiration

- Historical records and reports on the **Nakba (1948)**, the **Intifadas**, and the continuing **Gaza siege**.
- Human rights reports from **Amnesty International**, **Human Rights Watch**, and **UN archives**.
- Spiritual reflections from the **Holy Qur'an**, **Prophetic traditions**, and **Biblical imagery** that celebrate justice and steadfastness (*sabr*).
- The poetic legacy of **Mahmoud Darwish**, **Fadwa Tuqan**, and **Nizar Qabbani**.
- Contemporary writings and reports from **Al Jazeera**, **BBC Arabic**, and **The Guardian**.

Acknowledgement

The author extends heartfelt gratitude to all who preserve and share Gaza's truth — journalists, poets, and witnesses who speak when silence would be easier.

This book is dedicated to the people of **Gaza and Palestine**, whose courage, patience, and faith continue to inspire the conscience of the world.

1. "The Date Palms Remember"

(A Poem Inspired by the Treachery at Medina)

In the valley where treaties were sealed with words,
and the ink still glistened under the mercy of Medina's sun,
shadows whispered behind the walls.
Promises wore masks of peace,
while daggers hid beneath the robes of counsel.
They smiled with lips that knew deceit,
their tongues weaving silk and snare,
their hearts counting the coins of falsehood.
The Prophet's trust – a lantern in the dark –
was met with the breath of extinguishers.
But the earth had ears,
and the palm trees – silent witnesses –
heard the plotting beneath their roots.
The stones of Banu Nadir's fortresses
grew heavy with shame,

as betrayal bloomed where trust had been sown.
Then came the wind of justice,
a command carried on the unseen wings of decree —
no sword of men,
but the turning of destiny itself.
Walls that stood on lies crumbled,
and the proud were driven by their own shadows.
Yet the Messenger forgave where vengeance could rise,
and mercy stood like a green branch in a scorched field.
For truth does not shout —
it waits, it endures, it returns.
And today, the palms of Medina still stand,
their leaves trembling in the dawn wind,
whispering of the night when the veil of deceit was
torn,
and light walked out of the ruins.

2. “When Umar Walked into Jerusalem”

(A Poem of Justice and Peace)

He came not with chains, but with sandals of dust,
not with a crown, but with a heart that feared God.
The gate of Jerusalem opened – not to conquest,
but to conscience.
The stones, long soaked in centuries of pride,
watched in silence as a shepherd of justice entered,
his robe mended, his head bowed,
his soul carrying the weight of trust.
No sword sang that day,
no child wept behind walls,
for Umar’s step was softer than power,
and his command was the echo of mercy.
He said – *“This land belongs to all who pray.”*
And the bells of the Church of the Holy Sepulchre
rang beside the call of the muezzin,
as the Torah was read in peace beneath the same sky.
The Christians kept their crosses.

The Jews returned to their courtyards.
The Muslims bowed on the stones
that once knew the prophets' tears.
Thus, Jerusalem — Al-Quds — breathed again.
Not as a city of walls,
but as a garden of faiths,
where the covenant of Umar
was written not on parchment,
but upon the hearts of men.
And still, the olive trees whisper his name —
Umar,
who entered without pride,
who ruled without greed,
who guarded what was sacred,
and left behind
a justice the centuries still envy.

3. "When the Walls Wept"

(Jerusalem – Then and Now)

Once, a man entered Jerusalem barefoot,
and the stones rejoiced beneath his feet.
He carried no banner but the word of peace,
no promise but the covenant of mercy.
Now, boots trample where sandals once trod,
and the air trembles with the echo of walls collapsing.
Minarets and bells no longer share the wind –
their calls are drowned in the cry of mothers.
Once, the Church and the Mosque
stood like brothers on either side of dawn,
their prayers weaving a single song of worship.
Now, the streets are scarred with barbed wire,
and the holy ground tastes of smoke.
Once, Jews, Christians, and Muslims
drank from the same well of safety,
for Umar's hand wrote justice across their names.
Now, names are erased from doorways,

and homes crumble into silence.
Yet the city remembers –
it remembers the step of a Caliph
who refused to pray inside another's sanctuary,
lest history call it theft.
It remembers the parchment of peace
sealed not in ink, but in humility.
And the walls – yes, the walls – still weep,
for they have seen what men have forgotten:
that holiness cannot live in hatred,
and faith cannot bloom in fear.
But hope still lingers –
like a hidden root beneath scorched earth.
For the same God who watched Umar enter
watches now through the smoke.
And one dawn –
when the dust clears and hearts remember –
Jerusalem shall again greet its guardians,
not with war cries,
but with the whisper of angels:
"Peace be upon you – as it once was."

4. "The Crescent Over Jerusalem"

(The Crusades and Saladin's Justice)

Steel clashed with steel,
and banners bled across the hills of the Holy Land.
Cries of warriors echoed through valleys,
and Jerusalem trembled beneath the march of strangers.
Temples burned, churches trembled,
and the earth drank the sorrow of countless souls.
The invaders came with pride,
but left behind the taste of fear.
Yet in the midst of smoke and ruin,
a lion rose — not from vengeance, but from virtue.
Saladin, the just,
with eyes that measured mercy as carefully as might,
stepped into history's stage,
his hand steady, his heart bound to God's law.
He marched not to desecrate,

but to reclaim the sacred with honor.
No child was harmed; no priest expelled;
the defeated were fed, their wounds tended,
their dignity untouched by conquest.
When Jerusalem fell beneath his banner,
the city did not weep in humiliation,
but breathed again in relief.
For the Crescent had risen —
not as a shadow of tyranny,
but as the dawn of ethical triumph.
The Crusaders departed, their arrogance humbled,
their banners lowered,
while Saladin's words became legend:
"God does not love the oppressor,
and mercy is the crown of the just."
The olive trees remember,
the stones still whisper,
and the wind carries the tale:
that victory need not be cruelty,
that honor can outshine the sword,
and that faith, when bound to justice,
becomes the shield of nations.

5. "Echoes of the Lion"

(From Saladin to Gaza Today)

The lion once walked through Jerusalem,
not to crush, but to protect;
his banner rose like dawn over broken stones,
and mercy tempered the edge of every sword.
Centuries have passed,
and the olive trees still murmur his name,
yet the winds carry new cries –
children without homes, mothers without rest,
streets where laughter is a fragile bird,
easily silenced.
The walls remember Saladin's steps,
the echoes of honor in a time of war.
And now, Gaza bears the weight of history,
a land where courage is stitched with fear,
where every breath is a prayer,
and every heartbeat a testament.

The oppressors may rise,
their shadows stretching across rooftops,
yet the spirit of the Lion lingers —
in those who resist not with malice,
but with steadfastness, faith, and truth.
Let the world see Gaza not as rubble,
but as a land of ethical defiance,
where hope refuses to die,
and justice, though delayed, is never denied.
For the Crescent that once shone with mercy
still lives in the eyes of the faithful,
and the heart of the Lion beats
in every child who dreams
of freedom, dignity, and peace.

6. “When the Crescent Faded”

(Decline of the Ottoman Empire and Rise of British Rule in Palestine)

The crescent once ruled the sky of cities,
its shadow long over minarets and markets,
over olive groves and the laughter of children.
Ottoman banners fluttered in the wind,
not perfect, yet guardians of a land’s soul.
Time crept upon the empire,
its pillars cracked, its lanterns dimmed.
Governors grew distant,
and whispers of power reached foreign shores.
Then came the sea-born flags of Britain,
their sails heavy with ambition,
their treaties etched in ink, not in hearts.
Jerusalem, Gaza, and the hills of Palestine
breathed a new oppression,

their streets listening to strangers' commands.
The olive trees bent under new taxes,
the markets fell silent in the shadow of bureaucracy.
Yet in the homes and courtyards,
hearts whispered old songs —
prayers for justice,
stories of martyrs,
resistance sewn into every garment of memory.
The crescent faded from rooftops,
but it never left the skies of the soul.
For the people of Palestine knew:
even when banners fall,
even when foreign boots walk their streets,
their land remembers them,
and their spirit remembers the land.
The dawn will return,
and the crescent will rise again,
not as empire, but as hope,
for those who endure,
for those who never yield.

7. "The Promise That Burned"

(British Mandate and the Balfour Declaration)

A letter crossed the seas,
its ink heavy with ambition,
promising a land that was not theirs to give.
Palestine slept beneath ancient skies,
its olive trees dreaming in the moonlight,
while diplomats drew lines on maps,
blind to the heartbeat beneath the soil.
The Mandate arrived on iron boots,
their law written in foreign tongues,
their courts deaf to the prayers of mothers,
their soldiers blind to the cries of children.
Villages bent under new taxes,
markets grew silent under bureaucratic shadows,
and the land listened as strangers claimed what was not theirs.
Yet in homes and courtyards,
hearts whispered old songs —

prayers for justice,
stories of martyrs,
resistance sewn into every garment of memory.
The crescent faded from rooftops,
yet it lingered in the skies of the soul.
Even when banners fall,
even when foreign boots walk the streets,
the land remembers its children,
and the spirit remembers the land.
The promise of the oppressor burned,
but it could not burn the soul of Palestine.
Even in chains, even in exile,
hope grew stubbornly like a hidden spring,
waiting for the day the land remembers
its people, its dignity, and its free heart.

8. "The River of Exile"

(The Nakba)

The dawn broke over shattered rooftops,
and the streets whispered farewell to laughter.
Villages emptied,
and olive trees bent under the weight of sorrow,
their roots drinking tears of mothers,
their branches trembling with the cries of children.
A river of exile flowed through the hills,
carrying names, memories, and the scent of smoke.
Homes became dust,
fields became graves,
and the wind carried the echoes of promises
that never were.
They counted the stars and prayed for return,
but the earth beneath their feet
was claimed by strangers' papers and swords.
The sea received them in exile,

the deserts held them in silence,
yet their hearts remained in the land
that birthed them,
that held their stories,
that hummed with the songs of ancestors.
The Nakba was not a single day,
but a wound that spans generations,
a memory that refuses to fade,
a cry that echoes in every olive grove
and every hidden courtyard.
Yet the people endured —
their footsteps carved paths of resistance,
their prayers watered the roots of hope,
and their courage rose like a stubborn flame
against the night.
Palestine remembered them,
and they remembered Palestine.
The land may be divided,
but the heart of its children
remains undivided.

9. “The Land Between Borders”

(1948–1967 – Partition Aftermath, Jordanian/Egyptian Administration, and Refugee Crisis)

The map was drawn with rulers’ pens,
yet the land remained in the hearts of the displaced.
Villages vanished into whispers,
and olive trees stood as monuments to memory.
The refugees walked roads without names,
carrying the scent of homes they would never see.
Children slept beneath borrowed roofs,
and mothers sang lullabies to rivers of tears.
Jordanian hills welcomed some,

Egyptian sands held others,
yet everywhere the same longing endured:
a return, a remembrance, a justice deferred.
Borders on maps could not erase the soul,
and the wind carried the names of villages,
the songs of ancestors,
and the stubborn heartbeat of a people
who refused to vanish.

10. "Under the Iron Sky"

(1967 – Occupation, Military Rule, and Settlements)

The horizon darkened with armored wheels,
and the olive groves trembled under foreign boots.
Jerusalem, Gaza, the West Bank –
every street became a shadow of fear.
Settlements rose like thorns,
fences carved the land,
and checkpoints measured the breath of children.
Yet in the silence of courtyards,
in whispered prayers beneath shattered walls,
the people endured.
Teachers wrote lessons on rubble,
mothers planted hope in small pots,
and the youth's laughter defied the guns.
The land may be occupied,
the sky heavy with oppression,
but the spirit of Palestine

walks unseen paths,
carries its history in every heartbeat,
and waits for the dawn of freedom.

11. "The Voice of the People"

(Palestinian National Movement and Yasser Arafat)

From exile's dust to the streets of Gaza,
a voice rose over the rubble,
not of hatred, but of claim –
to a land remembered in heartbeats.
He walked with the weight of history,
Yasser Arafat,
wrapped in the keffiyeh of his people,
his eyes reflecting the generations of loss,
his voice carrying the prayers of the displaced.
Flags waved over villages and cities,
songs echoed through refugee camps,
and the world could no longer pretend
that a nation without a land is a nation without a soul.
The dream was not just for return,
but for recognition, dignity, and justice.
Even in exile, even under siege,

the people carried the torch:
their struggle written in every heart,
their hope rising with every dawn.

12. “The Stones Remember”

(Intifada and Ahmed Yassin’s Martyrdom)

The streets trembled with the rhythm of resistance,
stones in children’s hands,
prayers in mothers’ lips,
and the city itself rose in quiet rebellion.
Ahmed Yassin, the father of the steadfast,
walked with faith in his spine,
guiding the youth with courage,
a beacon amid the smoke and fear.
The oppressors’ guns roared,
tanks carved paths through alleys,
but the heart of Gaza refused to bow.
And when he fell, martyred by the cruelty of power,
the air itself seemed to mourn,
yet the flame he lit continued to burn:
in every whispered prayer,
in every stone thrown in defiance,

in every child who remembers that freedom cannot be silenced.

The Intifada is not merely revolt –
it is a story of endurance,
a chronicle of courage,
and a reminder that even in siege,
hope finds a way to rise.

13. "The Day the Silence Broke"

(The Breaking Point of a Besieged People)

For years, the walls grew higher,
the skies darker,
the sea closer yet unreachable.
An entire people lived between fences and fear,
their childhoods measured in blockades,
their dreams searched at checkpoints.
The world said, *"Be patient,"*
and Gaza tried.
Through rubble, through hunger, through grief,
they tried.
But patience has a sound —
the sound of mothers whispering prayers over dust,
the sound of children asking,
"Why does the world not see us?"
One morning, the silence broke.
Not in celebration,
not in victory,

but in a scream born of generations
who had been told to endure without end.
It was not glory –
it was grief overflowing.
It was not conquest –
it was a cry for existence.
And though the world will count headlines,
Gaza counts graves.
The powerful will write their reports,
but the powerless will write their truth:
that no soul can be caged forever,
and even the smallest breath of freedom
can shake the tallest wall.
So remember –
when the silence breaks,
it is not always war that speaks,
but the echo of the unheard.

14. "Before the Dawn"

(Children who wrote their will before martyrdom)

A boy of twelve wrote a letter before dawn –
not to his teacher, not to his friend,
but to the world that would not listen.
"My kite still flies," he wrote,
"and if it falls, let my brother hold the string."
He folded it neatly beside his schoolbooks,
as the sky rumbled with fire.
Another child whispered her will
into her mother's trembling hands:
"Don't cry for me,
plant a flower where I used to play."
And when the morning came,
they were gone –
their names etched not on gravestones,
but on the conscience of the earth.

The world read their wills too late,
but heaven heard them first.

15. "Alhamdulillah"

(Mothers of the Martyrs)

She stood amid the ruins,
dust on her hair,
a photograph in her hand –
the face of her son,
the light of her world.
The neighbors wept,
but she only whispered,
"Alhamdulillah."
Her voice did not tremble –
it rose like a prayer,
a declaration of faith
that even in grief,
she surrenders only to God,
never to fear.
"Allah chose him," she said,

"and I am honored."
And the wind carried her words
across the shattered streets,
so the world might remember
what strength looks like
in a mother's tears.

16. "The Last Broadcast"

(The Journalists, Medics, and UN Staff of Gaza)

The camera shook,
but his voice did not.
He spoke as the bombs fell,
turning rubble into testimony.
Each word was a shield,
each truth a defiance
against the silence of the powerful.
She held her microphone
with trembling hands,
her vest marked "PRESS" –
as if that could save her
from the bullets of fear.
They became witnesses
and martyrs of truth –
faces the world saw for a moment,
then forgot.

But Gaza remembers them.
The ink of their courage
stains the pages of history,

17. G — Graves

(Lives Lost, Martyrs, and Memory)

Beneath shattered rooftops and rubble-strewn streets,
sleep the children, the mothers, the fathers —
martyrs of a siege that never truly ends.
Their names are not written on stone,
but in the wind over olive groves,
in the songs whispered by those who remain,
in every heartbeat that refuses to forget.
The graves are many,
yet the spirit is one —
Gaza remembers,
and Gaza carries the fallen
in the marrow of its bones.

18. A – Ashes

(Destruction, Siege, and Suffering)

The sky rains fire,
the streets inhale smoke,
and homes crumble into memories.
Ashes settle on children's hair,
on mothers' laps,
on the fields where olive trees once sang.
Yet in the dust, life stirs –
a stubborn plant grows,
a mother teaches,
a child dreams.
Ashes do not bury hope;
they remind the world
that resilience blooms where fire falls.

19. Z — Zeal

(Resistance, Faith, and Enduring Spirit)

In courtyards, schools, and mosques,
the people of Gaza rise again.
Not with hate, but with courage,
not with vengeance, but with steadfastness.
Teachers, poets, mothers, youth —
their zeal becomes a shield, a flame, a prayer.
Every act of learning, of love, of survival,
is resistance.
Every heartbeat defiant,
every story told,
a victory of spirit over siege.

20. A — Ascension

(Hope, Rebirth, and Promise of Freedom)

One day the rubble will bloom again,
streets will echo with laughter,
and the horizon will shine with dawn.
Gaza will rise —
not in walls of stone,
but in hearts unchained,
in courage that refuses to bow.
The martyrs' whispers guide the steps,
olive trees wave like banners,
and the Crescent shines above,
a testament that the land remembers
and the people endure.

21. "G A Z A"

(Epilogue – The Soul of the Land)

G – Graves that blossom into gardens of remembrance,
where martyrs sleep beneath the weeping olive trees,
and the soil still hums their names to the wind.
A – Ashes of homes that once held laughter,
now scattered, yet sacred –
from their dust, new dreams take root.
Z – Zeal that burns brighter than bombs,
the faith of children who write their wills in notebooks,
of mothers who whisper "Alhamdulillah" through their tears,
of teachers who build classrooms in the ruins,
and poets who turn pain into prophecy.
A – Ascension – not just of bodies,
but of souls, of truth, of a nation unbroken.
Their spirits rise beyond the siege,
their courage pierces every blockade,
their prayers ascend where drones cannot reach.
Through centuries of conquest, betrayal, and blood,

they stood –
from Umar's justice to Saladin's honor,
from exile to intifada,
from ashes to defiance.
The world may count the dead –
but Gaza counts the steadfast.
The world may draw its borders –
but Gaza draws its breath from faith.
And when the last wall falls,
and the last tear dries,
the dawn will break again –
not red with fire,
but gold with return.
Because GAZA is not a place alone –
it is the pulse of a people,
the echo of endurance,
the living verse of a land
that refuses to die.

Author's Note

(Afterword to "G A Z A")

This book was not written — it was *wept.*

Each poem is a fragment of a cry that has echoed for generations,

a whisper from the stones of Jerusalem,

a tear from the eyes of a mother in Gaza,

a heartbeat from a child who learned courage before childhood itself.

When I began this journey, I did not seek to write history —

I sought to *listen* to it.

To the soil that still remembers its martyrs,

to the wind that carries their names,

to the olive trees that have witnessed both peace and fire.

Gaza — for many — is a name spoken with sorrow.

But for me, it became an alphabet of faith:

G — Graves that do not silence love,

A — Ashes that refuse to scatter,

Z — Zeal that burns through oppression,

A — Ascension that transforms pain into prayer.

The people of Gaza are not symbols — they are souls.
They do not seek our pity,
but our witness.
They do not call for sympathy,
but for truth.
This book is my humble offering to them —
to the children who wrote their wills with crayons,
to the mothers who say *Alhamdulillah* through grief,
to the journalists who filmed until their final breath,
and to every soul who stood, unarmed yet unbroken,
before the storms of our time.
If these poems stir a tear,
let it be one that waters the roots of remembrance.
If they spark anger,
let it be righteous — the kind that demands justice, not vengeance.
And if they awaken hope,
then may that hope rise like dawn over a land
that has seen too many nights.
Because Gaza is not a wound alone —
it is a witness.
And as long as one heart beats for truth,
Gaza lives.